Praise for Bruce Eric Kaplan and *I Was a Child*

"[Bruce Eric Kaplan's] memoir begins: 'I was a child, but I wasn't very good at it,' and if you get what he means, then this is the book for you. . . . In other words, he renders his family's peculiarities so perfectly that they become universal. . . . His recollections are never of anything extraordinary. They're deadpan, hilarious, and really quite moving." —*The Philadelphia Inquirer*

"[A] delightful memoir . . . [and] a funny and moving look at the figures that inspired Kaplan's cartoon world." —*The Wall Street Journal*

"If *The Little Prince* had crash-landed, instead of in the Sahara, into a middle-class Jewish home in Maplewood, N.J., in the late 1960s, it might feel something like *I Was a Child*." —*The Hollywood Reporter*

"*I Was a Child* made me so happy and so sad at once. It is a sweet and hilarious gut-puncher. That a memoir rooted in rage and confusion could leave me aching with love, determined to forgive, and desperate for seventies TV is glorious alchemy indeed."
—Maria Semple, author of *Where'd You Go, Bernadette*

"Bruce Eric Kaplan's beautiful memoir, *I Was a Child*, does what his deceptively simple drawings do: takes complicated feelings—here the baffling questions, the

confinement, and the secret freedom of childhood—
and makes them funny and unsettling and achingly
sad. Anyone who was a child will love it."

—Maile Meloy, author of
The Apprentices and *The Apothecary*

"The world according to Bruce Eric Kaplan is funny,
idiosyncratic, and heartbreaking. This memoir, with
his divine drawings, is so evocative that, though his
childhood was utterly unlike mine, it sent me careen-
ing down a memory lane of my own: my bedroom, the
breakfast table, the front steps to my house, what my
mother said, candy bars, favorite TV shows. Also it
made me cry."

—Delia Ephron, author of *Sister Mother Husband Dog*

"I read this book in a single sitting, laughing out loud
and quoting lines to anyone who would listen. It cap-
tures the deep strangeness and melancholy of childhood with sneaky accuracy and unexpected emotion,
as well as excellent cartoons."

—Tom Perrotta, author of *Election* and *Little Children*

"In his poetically illustrated memoir, Bruce Eric Kaplan
manages to capture all that is beautiful, hilarious, and
painful about growing up human. He will make you
laugh with recognition, cry with nostalgia and longing,
and somehow wish you were growing up bored in New
Jersey."

—Lena Dunham

"Bruce Eric Kaplan's prose is a lot like his drawings: blunt, arresting, and hilarious. *I Was a Child* is extremely entertaining and deeply upsetting, often simultaneously. I enjoyed every page and was sad when it was over."

—Simon Rich, author of *Ant Farm*
and *The Last Girlfriend on Earth*

"This is a wonderful, touching, and funny book."

—Roz Chast, author of National Book Award
finalist *Can't We Talk About Something More Pleasant?*

"Bruce Eric Kaplan had a childhood like no one else's, and his droll book demonstrates exactly how unusual it was. . . . The kind of upbringing you might associate with a character on *Seinfeld*. . . . [A] tender homage to his family, flaws and all."   —*The Washington Post*

"A wry, sharply observed memoir."   —*People*

"Bruce Eric Kaplan has written a hilarious, touching autobiography."   —*Entertainment Weekly*

ALSO BY BRUCE ERIC KAPLAN

CARTOON COLLECTIONS

No One You Know

This Is a Bad Time

I Love You, I Hate You, I'm Hungry

PICTURE BOOKS FOR CHILDREN

Monsters Eat Whiny Children

Cousin Irv from Mars

Meaniehead

PICTURE BOOKS FOR ADULTS

The Cat That Changed My Life

Every Person on the Planet

Edmund and Rosemary Go to Hell

Everything Is Going to Be Okay

I WAS A CHILD

BRUCE ERIC KAPLAN

BLUE RIDER PRESS

New York

blue
rider
press

An imprint of Penguin Random House LLC
375 Hudson Street
New York, New York 10014

The Library of Congress has catalogued the hardcover edition as follows:
Kaplan, Bruce Eric.
I was a child / Bruce Eric Kaplan
p.   cm.
ISBN 978-0-399-16951-9
1. Kaplan, Bruce Eric.   2. Cartoonists—United States—Biography.
3. American wit and humor, pictorial.   I. Title.
NC1429.K268A2   2015   2014027911
741.5'6973—dc23
[B]

Blue Rider Press hardcover edition: April 2015
Blue Rider Press paperback edition: April 2016
Blue Rider Press paperback ISBN: 978-0-399-18341-6

Printed in the United States of America
1   3   5   7   9   10   8   6   4   2

Original hardcover book design by Gretchen Achilles

Penguin is committed to publishing works of quality and integrity.
In that spirit, we are proud to offer this book to our readers; however,
the story, the experiences, and the words are the author's alone.

This book is for my
parents, who tried

I WAS A
CHILD

I was a child, but I wasn't very good at it. I'm not sure why. I think a lot of us are born waiting to be adults. I know I was. I just sat there, waiting. This is that story.

MY MOTHER went into labor with me at the 1964
World's Fair, which was in Queens, New York. Every
time I fly into JFK and take a cab to Manhattan, I look
out the window at the old fairgrounds and I think,
That's where I began.

I WAS TAKEN home to 20 Sommer Avenue in Maplewood, New Jersey. On the front porch was a gray box

meant for milk bottle delivery and pickup. When I was a baby, a milkman would come by once a week to pick up the old bottles and replace them with new ones. Then, of course, he stopped coming when all the milkmen stopped coming.

That box stayed on the front porch for the next four decades, empty. When something was put somewhere at my parents' house, it stayed there—long after it broke, or no longer served a purpose, or just wasn't used anymore for whatever reason.

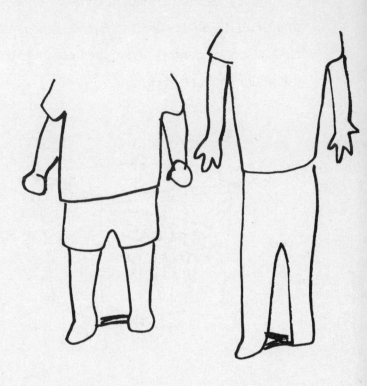

I HAVE two brothers, Michael and Andrew, seven and four years older. I have no idea how they felt about me showing up.

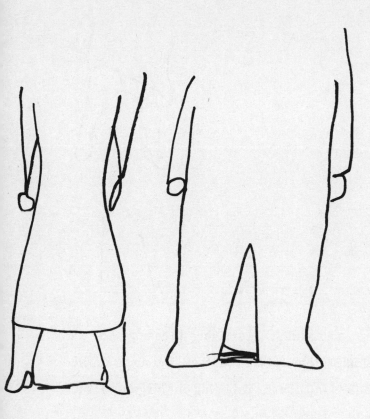

I do know that very early on, I had the sensation that everyone was a lot bigger and they could hurt me.

My MOTHER couldn't take having three boys. She was extremely jumpy, to say the least. Any noise startled her. The sound of a pot dropping on the ground could make her hit the ceiling.

"I'm getting discombobulated!" she would scream, when we were too loud or would be too much for her in some way.

She spent a lot of time being discombobulated.

WE HAD a hamster whom we named Hampy. One day, she somehow gave birth to baby hamsters and we clamored around her tank, looking at them. Then we watched in horror as Hampy ate all her babies. My mother told us it was because we scared Hampy.

I felt we were too much for Hampy, just as, apparently, we were too much for my mother.

ONE NIGHT when I was very little, I had a dream in which I saw a bee who started crying. I woke up very upset about the sad bee. I wish I knew why that bee was crying and why I was so sad that he was so sad.

My FIRST best friend was Majorie O'Malley, who lived next door. We got into a fight and she scratched my face. The scratch is still there.

The O'Malleys' house smelled different from our house. In fact, everyone's house had its own distinct smell. I was confused because that meant our house had a smell but I couldn't smell it.

IN OUR LIVING ROOM, there was an enormous dark piece of furniture. It was a cabinet with a built-in

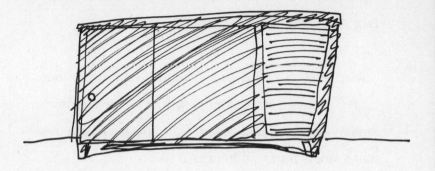

record player on the right side and a place to store records on the left side. I remember listening to a recording of "It's a Small World" and studying the album case. Much later, I would learn that "It's a Small World" was written for the 1964 World's Fair, and made its debut as a ride there. Maybe that's where my parents got it, just before I showed up.

Albums were mysterious objects that you studied over and over again, memorizing every single corner of them while you listened to the record. My parents had a copy of *My Fair Lady*. On it, there was a drawing of Rex Harrison pulling strings attached to Julie Andrews as if she was his puppet.

I was transfixed and horrified.

The record player broke shortly after I was a toddler and it was never fixed. That enormous dark piece of furniture stayed in the living room for the next twenty years.

When I got older, I was in charge of dusting the living room. Once a week I took the bottle of Pledge and a rag and dusted the cabinet with the record player that didn't work.

We inherited a piano when I was in junior high, and I dusted that every week, too. No one in my family could play the piano, and the piano arrived at our house out of tune and was never in tune. It was a place to put photos.

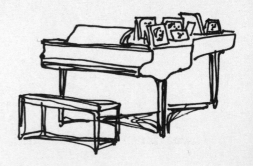

My mother's job was to take care of me and my brothers. My father's job was being a math textbook editor. He took the train into the city each day to go to work. My mother drove him to the train station each morning, and each evening, he walked home from the train. He usually caught the same train and always arrived home at the side door. So when the clock said six, I got in place at the top of the back stairs and waited for him.

My father always wore a hat to work.

Spring & Summer & Fall hat

Winter hat

WE WERE always told that my father wanted to be a short story writer or a novelist or a TV writer, but he had to give up his writing career for something more steady once he had a family. There was a box of his old writing in the attic. One piece was an unpublished short story about a man and a woman who fall in love when the woman's platypus escapes and the man finds it.

WHEN I was three I started preschool. It must have been only several times a week because when my kids started preschool, my father asked, "So, do they go two or three days a week?" I said, "No, every day."

For the next four years, anytime preschool came up, regarding my son, and then my daughter, my father would pause and say, "So, do they go two or three times a week?" Sadly, preschool came up a lot. "No, every day," I continued to say, during our weekly telephone calls. And then I would hold the phone away from my ear while he kept talking and would jump up and down with frustration. My wife wondered what the noise was the first time it happened, then got used to it.

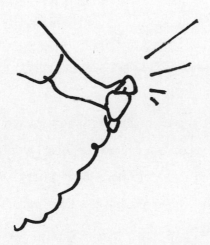

I SPENT a lot of time at the Maplewood Memorial Park playground. There were wooden logs to walk on there that I have never seen in any other playground.

I would think about those logs when I wasn't there. And when I was on my way to the logs, I would think, "*Soon I'm going to be on those logs.*" There's nothing better than having a purpose. I love purposes and hate vacations.

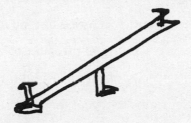

There was also a seesaw. You don't see seesaws as much anymore. It must be because the person on the bottom was always deciding to get off without telling you and you would crash to the ground and it would really hurt. It happened again and again and you just kept playing on the seesaw anyway.

ONE OF my earliest memories is sitting on my father's lap, watching *Here's Lucy,* a Lucille Ball situation comedy on CBS that began with a dancing little doll Lucy.

The credits would come on, and at the end, the little doll Lucy pulled back a stage curtain, revealing the real Lucy. Although I wasn't able to put it into words then, I think what I found so compelling about that moment each week was the expression of a truth—we are all just little dolls of ourselves who occasionally pull back the curtains to reveal the real us.

THERE WERE only two comfortable chairs in our den, where the TV was. Then there was one uncomfortable chair.

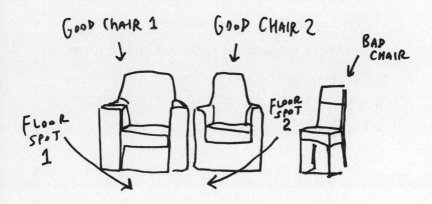

So if all five of us were watching, it would be two parents in the good chairs, one kid in the bad one, and two kids on the floor. If it was just the three kids watching, then two got the good chairs and one got the bad one. If you were in a good chair, under no circumstance could you get up, because then someone would take your good chair. If you had to go to the bathroom, you held it in.

MY MOTHER'S father was a furniture upholsterer. He upholstered the two comfortable chairs in the den and the comfortable chair and couch in our living room. On all of them, he put little sleeves that went over the place where you rested your hands. The thought behind it was that when they got dirty, you just put the sleeves in the wash. But in practice, they just got gray like the part underneath would have but didn't. Still, you had to have the little gray sleeve on at all times to protect the clean part underneath that you never saw.

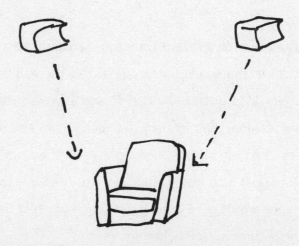

THERE WAS a big fan in the attic that you turned on and then left the door to the attic open. That was supposed to cool the house in the summer. It didn't.

THE DOOR to the attic didn't close right. You had to fold a piece of paper and stick it in the door at the exact right moment you shut it. That piece of paper was often on the floor next to the door to the attic because someone hadn't slipped it in at the exact right moment.

THERE WERE three bathrooms—the one off the kitchen, the one in the upstairs hallway, and my parents' bathroom. Like the door to the attic, the door to my parents' bathroom didn't close right. In this case, it was always just a tiny bit open, as if the door was just a little too big for the frame. Neither door ever got fixed. My parents believed in just living with things.

There was a bookcase in their bedroom that was set at an angle for no real reason. It was just floating. The bookcase had books my parents never looked at and old copies of *Reader's Digest* they never read.

EVERYTHING in our house was repaired with Scotch tape. If a paint chip was coming off, it was taped down. If there was a tear in a lamp shade, a piece of tape was put on it.

I felt held together by Scotch tape, and still do.

SINCE I was the smallest, I couldn't hit my brothers or I would get hit back. Once I got so mad I turned over the dining room table.

When guests came, we would pull either end of the table and put leaves in it and it would magically get bigger.

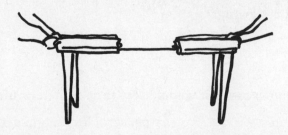

I WENT to Tuscan Elementary School. My mother walked me there for kindergarten. After the first year, you just walked with your friends on the block to school every day. At busy corners, there would be sixth graders who were crossing guards.

I spent my whole time at Tuscan dying to become a crossing guard. I did, ultimately. They gave you a red strap that crossed your chest diagonally, then went around your waist and was fastened with a big

buckle. I rolled it up carefully when I wasn't using it. It sat next to me at night on my dresser. I would fondle it lovingly.

IN KINDERGARTEN, we had rest time for ten or fifteen minutes. We rested on carpet samples that must have come from a local store. Once I fell asleep during rest time. Before I went to sleep, I was surrounded by my whole class on carpet samples. When I woke up, I was alone in an empty room, disoriented, seized with fear. It was as if I was the only person left on the planet. *No one else exists,* I thought. *Maybe I don't even exist anymore.*

YOUR FRIENDS were the kids who lived on your block. No one was driven anywhere for anything. Jeffrey Van Kirk had high hair that looked like it could topple off his head at any moment.

Bill Bigelow's mother screamed at her three sons. In the summer, everyone's doors and windows were open at all times, plus everyone was in their backyards all day and night. So we heard her screaming a lot. She was losing her mind having three boys, just like my mother.

WHEN I was very little, there were reruns of *The Donna Reed Show* and *Leave It to Beaver* in the mornings on TV. In these shows, there was a black-and-white world of loving mothers happily taking care of kids while the fathers were busy at work. It wasn't quite of our time, but it was still relevant.

Then suddenly these shows were all gone, replaced by *Get Smart* and *I Dream of Jeannie* and *F Troop*.

MY PARENTS never had parties. They had family gatherings. The only time I remember non–family members being entertained in our house was occasionally on New Year's Eve. The Riegels, a couple from across the street, would come over and we would bring out the plastic champagne glasses. I got Cheez-Its on New Year's Eve. Cheez-Its represented total, utter wild abandon.

ACROSS THE STREET from us lived Mrs. Soskin. She lived all alone in a big house, which looked less taken care of than the others on the block. There was a tall pine tree between our driveway and the O'Malleys' house. I would climb all the way to the top of it and watch Mrs. Soskin come out or go into her house. I never saw anyone else enter or leave her house, and that was sad for some reason.

I don't think Mrs. Soskin drove. She just did things in her garden. When I was alone at the top of the tree, everything got so still. I felt like I could really think up there.

AFTER SCHOOL, I played with my friends on the block. You went from house to house in the winter, yard to yard for the rest of the year. The afternoon went by very quickly, and suddenly it was dinnertime. You knew it was dinnertime because your mother went out the back door and screamed your name. That was the system. I remember being in the middle of a game, hearing my name, and just leaving. Someone was there and then they weren't.

IN THE WINTER, when it would get dark before dinnertime and you had to go inside to play, I might be able to watch TV at someone else's house. We would watch *The Munsters* at Jeffrey Van Kirk's house.

I never really got into *The Munsters* that much, but there was one aspect that was compelling. That was Marilyn. She was the only normal one among this group of creatures. Plus, she was really, really beautiful. And no one treated her as special. In fact, she seemed a little less-than for some reason. Not only did she accept this strange series of events, but she seemed to have great love for her family despite their strangeness. She didn't seem to resent them or be repulsed by them. I think this struck a chord with kids because maybe we all felt like Marilyn in *The*

Munsters. I know I did. And we struggled to not resent our families or be repulsed by them. Maybe we all ask ourselves, *How did I get put here with these people who aren't really people?*

I HAD a GI Joe doll because we all did.

We used to play with our GI Joe dolls in Jeffrey Van Kirk's basement, where his father had a workbench and various projects going on at all times. The idea of a father having a workbench was very wonderful and foreign to me.

MY FATHER had a secret toupee. My brothers found it once in a little box in the basement. It looked like a bird's nest.

He never wore it. I think he ordered it through the mail, then when it arrived, tried it on once and never had the nerve to wear it.

He was very self-conscious about being bald. He had two or three long strands of hair that began at the left side of his head and traveled over to the right side of his head so there would be hair on top. He still looked bald, but I guess in his mind he had come up with a way of tricking people that he wasn't, I guess. On a windy day, it looked bizarre.

MY BROTHERS and I had our own bedrooms. All five of us slept upstairs with our doors slightly open.

Often I would wake up in the middle of the night and be seized with the idea that my parents and my brothers had come up with a plan to run away. They had waited until I fell asleep, then quietly packed their things and snuck out.

I would be very still and listen for the sounds of their breathing coming from their rooms.

When I heard it, I could relax.

MY MOTHER went to a butcher once a week. Then, at a certain point, we started getting a box delivered to our house on Fridays filled with hamburger meat, roast beef, and chicken.

We had roast beef on Friday nights. When my mother took it out of the oven, she untied the bloody string that held it together, then cut it.

Once we ate a bum roast beef. It just didn't taste right. The next day, I remember my mother was on the way to take my father to the train station in the morning, walking down the back stairs. Suddenly, she turned around, ran back up the stairs, and pushed me aside to run to the bathroom off the kitchen. She had diarrhea. We all got diarrhea from the bum roast beef.

Sometimes when my mother was standing at the counter, rolling up raw meat to make hamburgers, she would make a little ball and pop it in her mouth like an animal.

In the winters, our radiators clanked and hissed, which is still the happiest sound in the world to me.

If you had a school project, you needed oak tag. Plus extra oak tag for when you messed up. All the way through high school, you still needed oak tag for school projects.

I made a lot of dioramas in elementary school, but not any in high school. Dioramas were always made out of old shoe boxes.

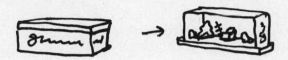

My dioramas always had leaves and pipe cleaners in them. No one ever talks about how odd it is that pipe cleaners come in many colors and are somehow art supplies when they are pipe cleaners.

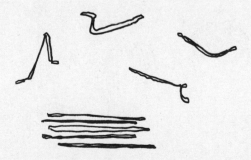

MY MOTHER had the same haircut from my earliest memory to when she died. She had the exact same haircut in her college yearbook and in her wedding photos.

It was like it was a birthmark.

MY BROTHERS and I always had bad haircuts. Not one good one. There was always too much hair somewhere or too little somewhere. I don't know why.

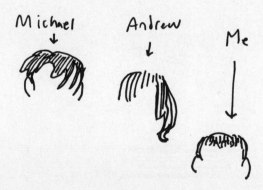

IN GENERAL at the time, there was so much hair everywhere. There was a character on *Room 222* named Bernie, and his hair was crazy.

I liked Bernie, but my favorite character on *Room 222* was Jason because the actor's name was Heshimu.

NEITHER OF my parents ever exercised, not once, that I know about. I didn't know anyone who had parents that exercised.

MY FIRST sexual moment was with a tree. Jeffrey Van Kirk's backyard bordered Mark Peto's backyard. There was a fence between them and a tree in Mark

Peto's yard that abutted the middle of the fence. We would climb the fence, go over to the tree, wrap our arms around it, then rub ourselves up and down the tree. We called it "The Tree That Gives You the Funny Feeling." When we touched the ground, we always ran to a red bucket behind their garages, and peed in it.

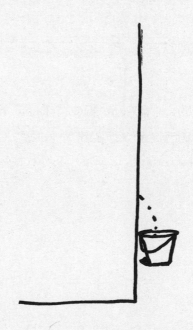

Mark Peto had an aboveground swimming pool.

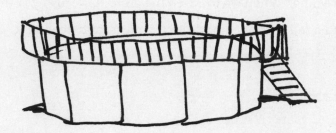

Since no one else I knew had a belowground or aboveground pool, I knew this meant he was very, very rich.

STORE WINDOWS were very confusing. Sometimes they would be bright and colorful and crowded. Other times, you would pass one that was sad and dusty and just had one little object, like a hat, in it. Or maybe just a hat and one faded hatbox.

EVERY TIME I went to the dentist I had several cavities. Today, my whole mouth is filled with lead.

You can see it if I open really wide.

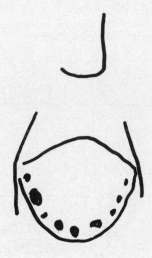

We walked up our street to go to the dentist. His office was a few blocks away in a little house. He spoke with a foreign accent and was definitely pure evil. When *Marathon Man* came out, I thought to myself, *I had one of those dentists.*

A trip to the dentist always ended with getting a ring from the same little dispenser. Year in, year out, there was never anything other than a ring.

NEAR the dentist's house was Springfield Avenue, which had little stores and shops that were never that clean. One was a little bakery that had pastries I loved. The pastry I loved the most was a cinnamon raisin swirly thing that the bakery ladies called a "melt-away." I have never heard of a melt-away since, but it is such a beautiful name and I think all things should melt away.

The dirtiest store was a candy and magazine shop right off Springfield Avenue. There was dust on every little object in that place.

The old man who sat behind the counter there was mean. It was strange that so many of the people who had jobs involving spending a lot of time with children seemed to hate children more than anything else in the world.

MY MOTHER thought our pediatrician Dr. Bootish was "very good-looking." It made me uncomfortable to have my mother think someone was very good-looking.

But I guess it was striking to see a good-looking person. There weren't that many good-looking people around for some reason. Maybe it was New Jersey or just who we knew. We would visit my grandmother in Forest Hills, Queens, on Sundays, and those people looked worse than the ones in New Jersey.

My father always made sure to bring a roll in the car to fortify himself during the journey to Forest Hills, which took less than an hour.

ONCE WE got stuck on the highway in an ugly stretch of Newark just past the airport. It was a hot day, and my mother suddenly said, "I'm dehydrating." She started to say it over and over again, "I'm dehydrating. I need water. I'm dehydrating." I had no idea what she meant initially, because no one ever talked about hydrating or dehydrating. We sat waiting in our Buick Skylark until finally some help came.

MY GRANDMOTHER ROSE lived in a two-bedroom apartment. The guest bedroom had a bed. That's it— no curtains, no table, no lamp. The bed had a bumpy white bedspread that made lines on your face if you lay down on it. There was something very scary and inhumane about that room to me.

The bed was on wheels like all beds. I never saw a bed that couldn't roll. Or one that wasn't covered by a bedspread.

My GRANDMOTHER had different milk than we did. It was called Tivoli. On the carton it said that Tivoli was "I love it" spelled backward, but it wasn't.

She also had Uneeda Biscuits, which weren't biscuits. They were actually thick crackers. "I needa biscuit," my brothers and I would all say to one another, over and over again, every week.

MY GRANDMOTHER and my father spoke of Barbra Streisand in a very serious way. It was because she had ascended to enormous heights despite the bigness of her nose, and all that it represented. Neither ever bought a Barbra Streisand album or tape, but we took my grandmother to Barbra Streisand movies. I don't remember ever taking my grandmother to a movie that didn't have Barbra Streisand in it.

Barbra Streisand's Nose

(around the time of
Funny Girl)

GRANDMA ROSE's husband died when he was in his forties. As far as I know, she never had a date or any romantic involvement after he died. I think I asked her about it one day or was in the room when someone did, and she said, "Eh, I did that."

She had a lot of friends and, of course, family. Sometimes someone would call when we were there. "Hello, darling," she would say to whoever it was, as she sat on the chair next to a table when you first entered. On the table was the heaviest black telephone in the world. The cord had black cloth to encase the wire. All old people had a table that was just for the telephone.

ONCE on our way to visit Grandma Rose, there was too much traffic at the Holland Tunnel so my father made a turn and tried to find his way to the Lincoln Tunnel. We drove around and around, until we arrived on a desolate street that seemed unconnected to anything.

"We're lost!" my mother said, upset and panicked.

A lone pedestrian appeared and my parents decided they would ask this very slow-walking man for directions.

We drove up next to him, and my father rolled down the window. You rolled down all windows by hand, obviously.

I looked at this man. He had a creepy hollow expression on his unwashed face, and his clothes looked like he had been wearing them for weeks. He was barefoot and was carrying a bucket of dirty dishwater.

Clearly, this man didn't know where anything was. No
one in their right mind would ask him for guidance in
any area. The only sane reaction to him would be to
drive quickly away.

Instead my father said, "Do you know how to get to
the Lincoln Tunnel?"

The man mumbled something incoherent. My father asked again. Again, the man mumbled something incoherent.

Then, finally, we just drove away. At that moment, I realized my parents really might not know how to do anything at all.

MY MOTHER's parents lived in West New York, which, oddly enough, is in New Jersey. I have a very vague memory of watching *The Ed Sullivan Show* in the living room of their small apartment. They kept what they called sucking candies in a thick glass bowl on the coffee table. My grandmother Fanny died when I was very young. My grandfather Abe had no teeth, not one.

Many other people must have had dentures, because there was a commercial constantly on television for Efferdent denture cleaner, which promised you could remove stubborn denture stains in minutes just by dropping a magical blue tablet in the glass of water holding the dentures.

GRANDPA ABE was also very, very deaf. "Papa," my mother would scream into the phone, when she called him. "Papa! Papa!" I don't remember anything else she said to him other than "Papa! Papa!"

He became increasingly forgetful. He left his car keys in his car one night, and when he woke up in the morning, the car was gone. He never got another car.

He lived his final days in a nursing home in Elizabeth, New Jersey, a town that had the worst chemical smell.

When I was little and we needed to drive through Elizabeth, I would pinch the end of my nose.

Then I got used to the smell. I wonder if they have figured out a way to make Elizabeth smell better now. I hope so.

WHENEVER we arrived home from visiting my grandparents or from anywhere at all that wasn't nearby, we would sing a song when we turned on our street and drove up to our house.

"We're here because we're here because we're here because we're here," we all sang. "We're here because we're here because we're here because we're here!"

And really that was the only reason we were here.

My mother had one fancy dress.

She wore it to all big occasions, which were either
a cousin's bar mitzvah or bat mitzvah or a cousin's
wedding.

I LOVED my mother's L'eggs containers. I wish everything came in L'eggs.

OUR KITCHEN CHAIRS started breaking. So my parents decided to saw off the chair part and turned them into stools. There were two gold balls on each chair that were always coming off. My whole childhood

was spent picking those gold balls up off the floor. My brother Andrew says we were told it was only going to be temporary, but it was permanent, like everything in our house.

EVERY stationery store had all the exact same candy, which you knew by heart, so it was very exciting when a new bar would show up.

The gum that came with baseball cards was always covered in white dust and was so brittle, unlike other gum. Sometimes you would open up the baseball cards package and the flat stick of gum would immediately break into little pieces, in which case you couldn't really chew it.

OLD MOVIES were on TV at all times of the day. The first one came on at ten in the morning on Channel 7. Channel 9 had the One O'Clock Movie, which had a lot of film noirs, the movies I loved more than anything. Channel 9 had the Four O'Clock Movie, which was John Ford Westerns or romantic comedies about nothing, starring someone pert like Janet Leigh. They still had thrillers sometimes, too, though. I loved *Midnight Lace* with Doris Day, who thought her husband, Rex Harrison, loved her, but really he despised her and was trying to drive her crazy and then murder her. There were a lot of old movies about how the person who was supposed to love you the most actually hated you enough to want you dead— those were my favorites.

CHANNEL 7 had the 4:30 Movie, which had a commercial every five minutes. The 4:30 Movie ended at six, so most movies would air in two parts. Some longer movies, like *The Great Escape,* would play in three parts, Monday through Wednesday. The 4:30 Movie was exhausting.

Often, the 4:30 Movie had a theme for the week, such as old strange Bette Davis week. *Whatever Happened to*

Baby Jane was on the first three days, then *Hush, Hush Sweet Charlotte* on the next two.

Those movies were so over the top and grotesque yet not exaggerated at all about the horrors of aging. My favorite week on the 4:30 Movie was James Coburn week. Monday and Tuesday would be *Our Man Flint*, Wednesday and Thursday would be *In Like Flint*, and Friday would be *The President's Analyst*, which never made any sense, probably because it had been chopped down to forty minutes.

I loved James Coburn because there was no one else in the world like him. He was so long. He seemed to go on forever.

AT EIGHT O'CLOCK, you could watch the Million-Dollar Movie on Channel 9, which had a lot of Fred Astaire and Ginger Rogers movies, or the WPIX Eight O'Clock Movie, which had more fun, frothy things, like *A Man Could Get Killed*, one of the many supposedly unfunny 1960s comedies I would watch that I would think were wildly hilarious.

Old movies played all night long on several channels. CBS had *The Late Show*, then *The Late Late Show*. Some movies would only play in the middle of the night, such as *Topper*. Topper was a guy who was haunted by Cary Grant and Constance Bennett, who had lives that were so wonderfully glamorous, being dead couldn't dampen them. They made being grown-up seem fun and exciting, in a way that none of the parents I knew did.

I remember coming downstairs at four a.m. once for some reason and seeing my father watching *Death Takes a Holiday*. I sat down and finished it with him, as the sun came up.

Weekends had movies all day and night, such as Creature Features, which had *Godzilla* or something actually scary. Sunday mornings always had an Abbott and Costello movie from 11:30 a.m. to 1:00 p.m. Their relationship terrified me.

Abbott seemed like he might have a violent side and could do anything if Costello provoked him too much.

IF YOU saw an old movie on TV and loved it, you knew
you could see it again, but you never knew when. It
might show up two months later or two years later.
There were a lot of movies I would wait for, checking
each week to see if they were back. I never missed an
Alfred Hitchcock movie. Never. I needed them. They
were all different yet beautifully all the same.

Alfred Hitchcock movies could be on any time of the
day or any channel. *North by Northwest* would be in two

parts on the 4:30 Movie on Channel 7. There was a moment where Cary Grant is in an elevator and his mother says to the two men who want to kill Cary Grant, "You're not really trying to kill my son," and then everyone except Cary Grant bursts into laughter. It was hilarious, and yet it was so upsetting that his mother didn't believe him. I could see one of my parents saying that to two hitmen who wanted to kill me.

Marnie would show up late Sunday afternoons on Channel 11, *Shadow of a Doubt* would be on the Four O'Clock Movie on Channel 9, *Foreign Correspondent* would only be on Channel 2 in the middle of the night, and all the early British ones would be on Channel 13 on a Saturday around nine p.m.

Saboteur aired on the One O'Clock Movie on Channel 9, so I could only see it if I was sick or had no school that day for some reason. *Saboteur* had the wonderful urgency of a World War II film. There was no urgency like that kind of urgency.

Even little Bob Hope light comedies that took place during World War II had that urgency. There was one Bob Hope World War II movie that I loved and would always wait for when it would be on again. It was called *They Got Me Covered* and in the middle of it, something terrible happened. A beautiful woman covered in pom-poms is on stage singing a song called "Palsy Walsy." The spies are in the audience and know they have to kill her before she can "talk." World War II movies were always about people not being allowed to talk.

The beautiful woman tosses pom-poms out into the audience while she sings. The spies catch one, stick a dagger in it, then throw the pom-pom back at her, stabbing her in the heart. She goes offstage and dies in Bob Hope's arms, before she can tell him whatever the spies didn't want her to. It was all very tragic for many reasons. The pom-pom lady had so much pathos even before she died for talking. You knew she wasn't going to get Bob Hope because he already had Dorothy Lamour.

And maybe worst of all, it was clear she was never going to achieve her show-business dreams beyond being a pom-pom lady.

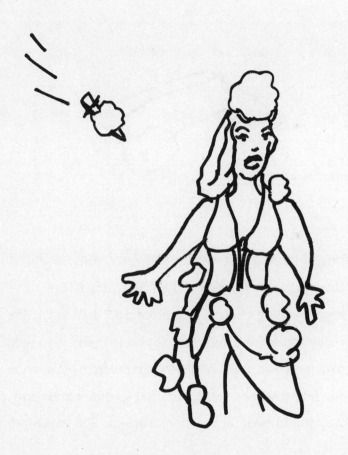

THERE WAS never any butter in our house. Just margarine. My parents acted like butter was lethal. I don't think I ever saw either have one piece of butter. I would go over to friends' houses and down sticks of butter.

THE ONLY TIME my mother was really relaxed was at the end of the day, when she was sitting in the living room, reading a book and smoking a Salem Light. She really earned that cigarette after a long day of having to clean, cook, and just deal with the three of us while my father was at work. She had a square glass ashtray she always flicked her ashes in. She looked so

happy carrying her ashtray into the living room. I
would give anything to have that ashtray now.

IN JUNIOR HIGH SHOP CLASS, I made an ashtray. I took
a square piece of metal, pounded dents into it, then
took four pennies and melted them so each penny
could hold a burning cigarette. It wasn't my idea—it
was my shop teacher's. I think he spent two decades
making thousands of these ashtrays for kids to bring
home to their parents.

MY MOTHER'S cigarette stubs always had a trace of the red lipstick she wore.

If you weren't looking at her, you could hear my mother smile because her lipstick cracked. I miss that sound.

I BELIEVE my father once told me that my mother had had one abortion before they married and one after me.

So there could have been five of us, I suppose, which really would have driven her mad.

THE BENEDETTOS lived next door. Mr. Benedetto started to rebrick the steep steps to their front door and for some reason stopped. So they had a front door you couldn't get to. There was a pile of bricks for years and years next to an empty space where steps should have been but weren't.

Since no one used the front door, everyone used the side door, which you could see from our living room, dining room, and den. The Benedetto daughters were older and pretty, and seemed to live a very glamorous

life when they came skipping home at eight o'clock
at night.

MY FATHER told me the facts of life when I was five
or six. We were watching *Julia*, a half-hour TV show
about a single mother played by Diahann Carroll who
worked for a kindly dentist.

My brothers kept saying she couldn't have a kid if there was no husband. "Why not?" I said, over and over again, until finally my father took me to the back stairs off the kitchen and sat me down on the red steps. "Bruce," my father said in his voice, which always got insanely deep when he was very serious. "When a man loves a woman, he puts his seed in her and they create a child."

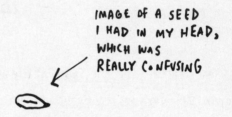

IMAGE OF A SEED
I HAD IN MY HEAD,
WHICH WAS
REALLY CONFUSING

I had no idea what he was talking about. Later, in second grade, I was playing at my friend Ricky Bergen's house after school. He slept in the same bed as his much older brother, who had a girlfriend.

Ricky took me under the picnic table in his backyard on a fall day and we sat in the leaves and he explained what his brother and girlfriend did. First, she played with his penis with her hands, which blew my mind. Then they had intercourse. He showed me what that was by taking a thin broken tree branch and putting it through the hole in the middle of the picnic table. He did it over and over again.

That was a much more helpful explanation than my father's.

WHEN YOU were sick, you stayed home and watched TV all day. Especially game shows. Sometimes a new game show would show up, then go away quickly. One I loved was called *The Neighbors,* on which a group of five neighbors were tested on secrets that they did or did not know about one another's marriages.

Another one, *The Magnificent Marble Machine*, featured an enormous pinball machine and that was stupid.

The Money Maze was a strange, sad game show that was on briefly. The idea was a couple had to navigate their way through a maze to get money, but the interesting part was that only one of them was in the maze. The other was on a perch above, telling them where to turn. One was always getting mad at the other one, either for not really listening or for telling them to do something they shouldn't. It was very, very true to life.

Our house was always cold. My father never let the thermostat go above 65. It started during the energy crisis, but then after the energy crisis it never went back up. He walked around the house in a scarf and tucked his pants into his socks so his body would feel the draft less.

My father was constantly having hot liquids, mostly tea. My mother had a lot of tea, too. Used tea bags would sit on little plates, quickly turning brown.

MY MOTHER was the worst cook in the world. After every single meal, my father said, "That was delicious." He would add, "Wasn't it, boys?" And we would say how delicious it was, too. We never ate out, except occasionally at Gary's on Springfield Avenue, where we ate burgers. When I got to college and had my meals at the campus cafeteria every day, I discovered how delicious food could be. I loved the salad bar, which featured small cut-up raw broccoli. I don't think I had ever tasted broccoli before, and it was amazing.

The only vegetables in our house were carrots and peas that came from cans.

EVERY DINNER at our house began the same way. We were called to come in. Then we all sat at the table, while my mother scurried around doing some last-minute things to get the food ready to bring to the table. Just as she would bring what seemed to be the last dish and sit down, she would leap up remembering one more thing, like a small dish of mayonnaise. The four of us would sit there, waiting. The rule was no one was allowed to serve themselves until everyone was seated at the table.

"Where's Mom?" my father would say in a booming voice over and over again. "Where's Mom?"

She was only a few feet away, dumping mayonnaise into a dish in front of his eyes, but still he kept saying "Where's Mom?" Something always became increasingly aggressive about his "Where's Mom?"

I don't remember the three of us ever answering his rhetorical question. I'm not sure I have ever understood why rhetorical questions exist, why people say them, or why there is a name for them. They should be outlawed.

Once my brother Michael made the mistake of helping himself to a piece of food before my mother had sat down for the last time. Maybe he couldn't help himself because it was steak—a meat we were served rarely. Everyone acted like steak was gold. Maybe they still do.

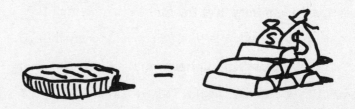

In any case, while my father was saying "Where's Mom?" Michael put the piece of steak on his plate. My father, quicker than I had ever seen him move, snatched it up in a fit of anger and threw it across the room toward the little white plastic garbage can that lived in front of the dishwasher.

He missed.

Everyone was very upset about the whole incident—most upset were my father, Michael, and my mother, who instantly broke into tears.

OLD CARTOONS were on before school—*Mighty Mouse, Bugs Bunny, Underdog,* and *Magilla Gorilla. Magilla Gorilla* opened with a bouncy song while Magilla got up for the day in the store he lived in. But the store had no insides. You could see the city behind Magilla Gorilla.

This gave me a very creepy feeling. He seemed exposed. Anything could happen to him in that store, which was supposed to protect him.

I WAS A CHILD

The *Magilla Gorilla* song was amazing. So many of my shows had amazing opening songs. *Nanny and the Professor* may have had the best one.

On the weekend there were new cartoons like *Jonny Quest* or *Josie and the Pussycats*. At the end of the summer, there would be a nighttime half-hour preview of all the new cartoons that would be starting the following Saturday morning, and that

87

was thrilling. Most of the new ones didn't last, such as *Hong Kong Phooey*.

There were always cartoons about people you would see in real life, like the Jackson Five or the Brady Bunch or the Harlem Globetrotters. I watched those ones, but they made me feel weird. I was happy when

the show would get canceled and the people would go back to existing in real life.

THERE WERE no cash machines and very few drive-through windows. You knew every single person who worked at the bank.

THE MUSIC TEACHER at Tuscan was a lady who came and taught us "Ta" and "Ti." She sat in a kid's chair and clapped her hands at us, chanting, "Ta Ta Ti Ti Ta, Ta Ta Ti Ti Ta, Ta Ta Ti Ti Ta!"

SOMETIMES you would be in your class and hear that there was going to be a fight after school. All day everyone would be abuzz about it. Then it would happen and be over in five seconds. Either some adult would break it up or, more often, it just ended.

Once I was one of the two kids who were going to fight. The other was Jesse Muir, who everyone called Fissy. We couldn't figure out where to have the fight at first. So we drifted from spot to spot, a trail of kids following us. We ended up doing it at his house. There was no front yard like everyone else had. There were just weeds and spider plants, some dead, and a lot of empty spider-plant pots. It indicated something not good to me.

The fight began and was over in five seconds like all the others. When I came home less than two minutes later, my mother was weeping. Parents knew about this kind of thing very quickly.

She was very, very, very upset—it was as if I would never get into college because Fissy and I had fought for five seconds.

Oh, brother, I remember thinking. I knew in that moment that neither she nor my father could ever handle knowing the truth about anything.

And they couldn't. They had no idea we played at the Maplewood Country Club golf course, which was near our house. It had the greenest grass I had ever seen.

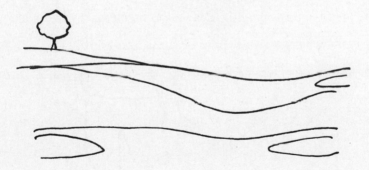

I ALWAYS think golf courses could be the most beautiful places in the world if you took away the golfers.

We roamed the golf course after school, running through the giant pipes that went underground from stream to stream. My mother would die again right now if she knew.

Anytime there was a house under construction, we played in it like it was a jungle gym when no one was there. I love the smell of sawdust, not that I would ever like to do any activity that creates sawdust.

Nails were everywhere, but if you stepped on one, you just bled for a bit, then moved on.

ALL OFF-LIMITS places were explored. I loved crawl spaces under people's houses, and still do. I wish I could crawl under your house right now.

THERE WAS a place we called The Forest between two streets a block away. On my street our backyards bordered other backyards on the next street over and everyone could see everything from yard to yard. The Forest was an enormous space of bushes and shrubbery between two backyards.

We would get lost in it for hours.

The strange thing was I went back to The Forest a few years later and I couldn't find it. It was just gone, as if we had dreamed it.

The day always ended the same way. I heard my name being called and ran home. My mother would ask me what I had done all afternoon. "Nothing," I always said.

She would purse her lips, wipe her hands on the dish towel she always carried, then go back and finish making dinner.

IF WE were playing in my house or yard after school, every now and then my mother would burst in, sniffing, and say, "Are you playing with matches?"

Sometimes we had been. Matchbooks were around everywhere. Not only did every business have a matchbook, but also there were tons of matchbooks offering ways of improving your life. A matchbook could change everything for you.

CINDY SNEIDER was a girl at Tuscan who was extremely in love with me for years. It was a deep love and I did nothing to create it. Once I got slightly injured at school and Cindy Sneider wept and wept. I don't expect to be loved that way ever again. We called her Snite Bite.

THERESA SERRANO was a girl who seemed to have a difficult time for one reason or another. Once she came up to the teacher and said, "My tushie's bleeding." This poor girl had to hear those three words over and over again for years.

I ALWAYS woke up excited to start the day. I am still that way. I am always excited for the next thing, whatever the next thing is—sadly, this can happen after starting what had just been the next thing moments earlier. I often start thinking about what I will have for dinner as soon as I take my first bite of lunch.

Sunday mornings, I always woke up excited to go downstairs and watch TV before everyone else was up. Sometimes *Davey and Goliath* would be on, which was a very moral show. Davey would do something wrong and his dog, Goliath, would say, "DAYVeeeeeey,"

in a very disappointed way. Then his parents would find out and give him a lecture with their beautiful weird claymation mouths.

After *Davey and Goliath* came *Wonderama*, which had a host named Bob McAllister. Basically, you watched him play games with the audience of children who came to the show. Bob McAllister often seemed to be pissed that he was playing games with an audience of children.

He had the longest microphone in the world, and you knew he wanted to hit someone with it.

A FEW years later came *The Patchwork Family*, which had a lady puppeteer. There were a lot of lady puppeteers—Kukla, Fran, and Ollie introduced movies on CBS on Saturday afternoons, and Shari Lewis and Lamb Chop were on different talk shows all the time.

My uncle Joel was proud that he once knew Shari Lewis. "She went to my high school," he would say. "I know," I would say. "You told me."

THE WIZARD OF OZ was on TV once a year. It was like Halloween or Christmas. You waited for it. And then a week or two before, you knew it was coming and thought about it a lot. Our first television was black-and-white, so I never knew Oz was in color, and had no idea the horse of many colors was changing colors. It didn't make a difference.

Once someone called during *The Wizard of Oz* and we all looked at one another, thinking, *Who would call during* The Wizard of Oz?

There was no voice mail, no answering machines. If you didn't answer, you never knew who it was. "They'll call back" was a big expression.

And later, the next time the phone rang, you would answer and say, "Did you just call?" We had one telephone number, like everyone else we knew. There were two extensions. One was on the wall of the kitchen and the other on the night table beside my father's bed—my parents slept in two twin beds pushed together. You always knew exactly how far each telephone cord could stretch. So if you wanted to answer the kitchen phone and still see the television, you could quickly run and get it, then pull it to the den. But you would only make it to the dining room and had to hold your head a certain way and look at the TV from there.

Plus, you would lose your seat to whoever may have been sitting on the floor. Oftentimes, someone upstairs would answer the telephone and someone downstairs would answer it. "Hello?" one would say. "Hello?" the other one would say when they picked it up right after. Usually it was a kid for me or for my brothers, and in that case, if my father was the other person to answer, he would stay listening until you screamed, "Hang up!" You knew it was him because his breathing was so loud. Sometimes you would have to say "Hang up!" several times.

I don't remember my father's mouth ever being completely closed, except for split seconds when he chewed something. Otherwise it was always hanging open.

Long-distance phone calls were only ever made after eleven p.m., when the rates changed. The only excuse for talking to someone who didn't live locally before eleven p.m. would be a crisis of epic proportions.

NOT ONLY was our TV black-and-white, but certain stations didn't come in well, so you were constantly adjusting the antenna. Someone told us to add tinfoil to the antenna, so we rolled up some and added it, but that didn't seem to help.

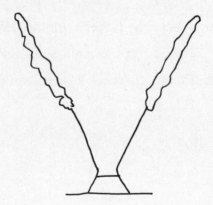

WHEN my mother drove, it was nerve-racking. It was as though she had an eight-hundred-pound weight on her foot at all times, speeding up and screeching to a halt at every stop. If a block was short, it felt like she was speeding up and slowing down at the same time. Sometimes, even now, I still feel like I am in that car.

When someone cut my mother off, she would say, "Oooooh—you, you dumb bunny!"

She couldn't bring herself to say something worse.

EVEN IF she wasn't driving, it was harrowing to be with my mother. When we would walk somewhere, she would suddenly shriek, "Watch out for the dog BM!" as if you would explode if you stepped on it.

Not stepping in it

If she didn't shriek that, she would shriek, "You stepped in the dog BM!" with the same end-of-the-world feeling.

Stepping in it

My brother Andrew supposedly stepped in dog BM so much that Michael said he had "the magnetic foot."

MY MOTHER gave out pencils for Halloween. And sometimes Trident gum. She didn't approve of candy. "The kids tell me they appreciate it," she would insist, despite how hard it was to believe.

We trick-or-treated right after school and were home before dark. When kids came to our door at night, I felt bad for them. They seemed to be leading very dangerous lives in which things were terribly out of control.

There was one candy that you always got on Halloween and that no one I knew ate.

I still don't know what a Mary Jane is, but I know it's bad.

FOR AT LEAST five years, this paperback book sat on my mother's bedside table:

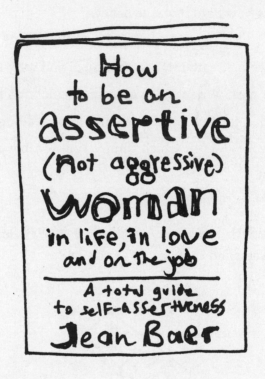

I am not sure if she read it.

MY PARENTS had this book in the living room:

Every Jewish person we knew did.

I NEVER went to one birthday party where anyone was hired to do anything. For a friend's birthday in second grade, his father took three of us to lunch at Burger King.

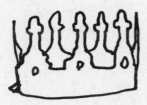

I was only invited to that kid's birthday once. I was in his class that year and was his friend. Then summer came, and the following year I wasn't in his class, so I stopped being his friend. That's a real life lesson, but I am not sure what the lesson is. If anyone knows, please tell me.

LIGHTNING BUGS came during the summer. We put holes in jars and ran around capturing them.

Sometimes the lightning fell off the bug, and that was sad.

I feel a little weird when people call lightning bugs fireflies.

IN THE SUMMERS, Tuscan school would have some sort of program in which teenagers would teach you things. I made tons of God's eyes each summer. After a while, the yarn would droop.

THE PROGRAM at Tuscan was only for a few hours. So every afternoon we would go to the Maplewood Community Pool. It was so, so crowded in that pool. It was like living inside a Richard Scarry book.

overhead view of pool

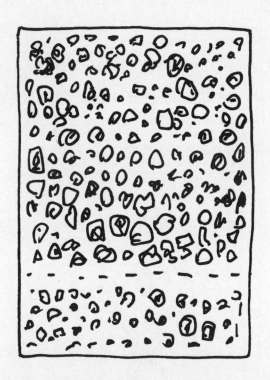

Then some kid would have an accident and the pool would quickly get evacuated.

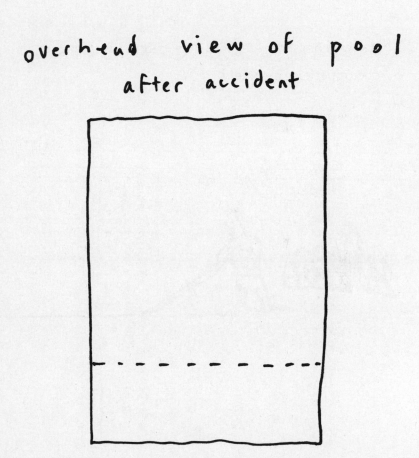

overhead view of pool
after accident

It had been total noise and chaos, and now it was all quiet and very still as a lifeguard fished a little brown turd from the bottom of the kids' end of the pool. I don't know why it stayed at the bottom instead of floating, but it did.

We watched the lifeguard like people watching a doctor perform a surgery.

Then the pool would go back to being a Richard Scarry book.

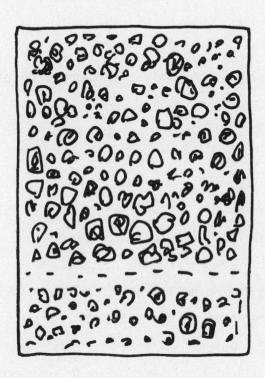

IN THE SUMMERS, three movies would be shown outdoors in Maplewood Memorial Park. The names of the three movies and the three dates they would be shown would be posted on a colored flyer on a community bulletin board in the park.

Thoroughly Modern Millie was usually one of the movies. And they showed *The Russians Are Coming, The Russians Are Coming* more than once.

We dutifully went to every one of the movies, getting there early, sitting on our blanket, and waiting for nightfall. Then the movie would start and you would never be able to hear anything. It was like they were talking through water. Drive-in movies were the same way. The sound was never right. You sat in your car, straining to figure out what the actors were saying. "What did he say he was going to do?" someone would ask. "I don't know," someone would answer.

I remember one drive-in movie where I was struck by the fact that we were all pretending that this was a good experience, but it wasn't. That became a very familiar feeling.

The most exciting moment of the occasional night-time drive home from Grandma Rose's was being on the highway in Newark and seeing the Bruce Lee movies playing on the drive-in from afar.

I never liked going to drive-in movies. I loved going to theaters, which were like magical temples. They were the most beautiful old buildings, with incredible moldings I would run my fingers over. The walls had murals, the ceilings were ornate, and the lighting was soft, coming from delicate wall sconces.

As soon as you entered a theater, you were enveloped with the most soothing old smell, mostly of pop-corn.

THERE WERE very few Disney movies, only old ones that would come back. And no new animated ones, just occasionally a new live-action one with Kurt Russell, like *The Computer Wore Tennis Shoes*. One summer I saw a commercial on TV for *The Parent Trap*. It was about Hayley Mills suddenly learning that out there, there was another her, which seemed like the greatest discovery of all time.

I begged and begged my father to let me go see *The Parent Trap*. I guess he really didn't want to go, because he finally said to me one day, sadly, "I wish I could take you, but it's rated X."

"Oh," I said, and dropped the subject. I knew that to take a kid to a movie rated X would be the worst thing anyone could ever do, actually against the law.

Years later, *The Parent Trap* came on TV and we watched it together. He loved it.

MOST SUMMERS, we took a two-week vacation where we would drive around New England and go see tourist attractions. We never missed a cavern.

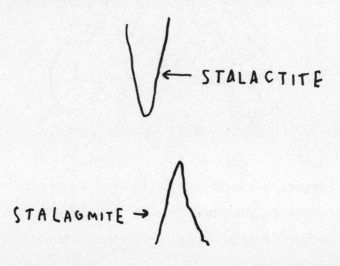

When things got crazy in the backseat, my father would say, "I'm going to pull over to the side of the road unless everyone stops that right now!" It was as if nothing could be worse than pulling over to the side of the road. But to tell you the truth, I do believe nothing could be worse. If you pull over to the side of the road, then you can't get to where you want to go.

I remember being in a gas station and looking at other families parked at the other pumps, studying them. They seemed like real families and we seemed like we were pretending to be a real family. They were always in a station wagon.

WE SPENT a lot of time wondering if the motel rooms we would stay in would have Magic Fingers, which was a little box you put a coin in, then the bed shook for a few minutes.

SOME OF the rest stops had Moo-Cow Creamers at the tables. You could buy Moo-Cow Creamers at the cash register. I begged for a Moo-Cow Creamer, but my parents wouldn't get one.

Once I found a Moo-Cow Creamer up the street, magically sitting on a pile of someone's trash on junk day. I grabbed it.

When I came home with my Moo-Cow Creamer and told my mother where I got it, she said, "That's disgusting," and made me put it in our pile for junk day.

SUMMER NIGHTS you would watch reruns, but also summer TV series, which were more casual than regular TV shows. There were a lot of variety shows starring couples.

My favorite was *The Melba Moore–Clifton Davis Show*, which began magically on a rooftop set.

The summer variety shows were light and fun, sort of sexy, almost drunken—they were what all summers should be.

When I was a little older, I watched *That's My Mama*, starring Clifton Davis, which I loved, but it just wasn't the same.

In the summer, networks would show the pilots of series that didn't get to be fall TV series. I loved those pilots and watched every one. You always understood why they never got to be a real TV show.

I loved TV. I wanted to crawl in the TV and stay there permanently.

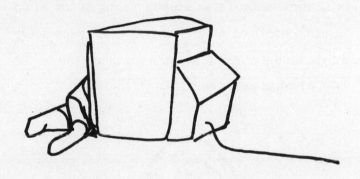

I guess in a way when I grew up and became a TV writer, I finally did.

At the end of summer, we made a trip to Maguire's, a small store in Maplewood, to get new clothing for school. It was as if that was the only time you grew. And we went to Millburn to Stride Rite to get Buster Brown shoes. I never understood who Buster Brown and his dog were, or what Buster was winking about.

IN SECOND GRADE, I was singing a song onstage in a Tuscan school assembly when suddenly I felt a heavy weight on top of me. It was the kid above me on the riser, who had passed out.

It was the first time I realized anything can happen—anything.

I THINK it was in second grade that I saw a production of *Hansel and Gretel* at Maplewood Junior High. The witch was played by my brother Michael's friend Cathy Payson. As soon as Cathy Payson came onstage, I was driven mad by fright. I cried and cried at how scary she was. I had to be taken out to the junior high lobby. Nothing could console me. Afterward, my mother thought it would help for me to see Cathy Payson without her witch makeup and nose so I would know that the witch wasn't real.

on stage   off

It didn't help. The truth is, I was experiencing the genuine horror of the story of Hansel and Gretel. Seeing Cathy Payson wasn't going to do anything.

The horror contained in the story still existed—it was much bigger than Cathy.

THERE WAS a commercial on in the mornings during *Green Acres* or *Petticoat Junction* in which a beautiful woman takes a bus to the Ritz Thrift Shop. A narrator explains some women sell their used furs there, others buy them. The woman tries one on and looks at herself in the mirror, happily transformed into a more moneyed person. She exits the store in her new coat and the narrator says, "You don't need a million to look like a million." The woman turns and says, "Oh," with incredible delight, then, "Thank you."

Every time it came on, I was mesmerized by it. It was a very powerful message—this idea that you could change your situation, you didn't have to settle for what you had, you could become more than what you were.

WHEN I was in third grade, my mother went back to work, and now my father was working from home. So he was in charge of my lunch. The options became a little more limited. Every day I had the exact same thing—one can of SpaghettiOs, into which I would dip several pieces of Wonder bread to soak up the tomato sauce.

I got fat.

MY FATHER hated a woman named Regina Schnitzer. No one knew why, not even him. Apparently, she had never done anything to him personally, but he despised her. We talked a lot about Regina Schnitzer, but now I don't know how we knew her or who she was. Maybe she lived in Maplewood, maybe she was someone he had worked with once—I just don't know and never will.

WE SPENT an inordinate amount of time at Tuscan talking about Thanksgiving, almost as if that was the only thing we spent time on. Each year we relearned Thanksgiving.

Now, each year my kids relearn Martin Luther King.

FREEDOM

They know more about Martin Luther King than anyone or anything else.

Tuscan looked like every other elementary school in Maplewood and South Orange. I suppose they were all Tudor. I thought it was very beautiful. The halls were enormous and the bathrooms had high ceilings. We would fold paper towels into squares, wet them, and throw them up at the ceiling, and they would stay there.

THE GYM at Tuscan had the most wonderful orange wood floor. The light in there was always orange, which, now that I think about it, was because of the floor. At the time, I didn't realize that. I just knew at the end of gym, it would be sort of sad to come out into the world where the light was normal. I hated gym, though, of course. I never got all the way up the knotted rope that didn't feel like rope because I guess it was covered with some kind of plastic. It reminded me of my uncle Martin's couch, which didn't feel like a couch because it was covered in plastic.

THE DESKS at Tuscan were covered in carvings, and people had written things on them. There was hardened gum and glue and other things stuck underneath them.

Each desk had a hole toward the upper right meant for an inkwell, which we didn't have. We just threw things into the little hole.

Every classroom had a cloakroom, where you would put your coats, since no one had cloaks.

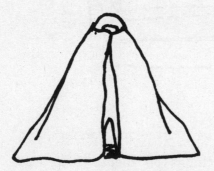

MRS. SARNO was my fifth-
grade teacher. She was angry
and seemed to hate children.
She smelled bad when she
came back from her cigarette
break down the hall.

WHEN YOU watched Channel 13, the public TV station,
you had to play with the antenna more than usual.
But nothing ever really helped. You always got a
double image. Everyone looked like they had a ghost.

There were a lot of televised plays, most of them on Channel 13. Televised plays had an ominous quality. They were always on tape, not film, so things echoed. And people wandered around on what were clearly sets instead of life, and this made them all seem a little like they were trapped in a *Twilight Zone* episode.

One play I watched on Channel 13 was called *Monkey, Monkey, Bottle of Beer*. It took place in the waiting room of a clinic, where four or five mothers sat talking while their kids were inside being examined by doctors. All the kids were mentally challenged in some way, and the doctors were going to figure out which ones would be selected for a magical treatment that would cure them. Or something like that.

The pain of *Monkey, Monkey, Bottle of Beer* was almost too much for me. I remember barely being able to walk once it was over. I still think about those poor mothers, hoping their children would be different. I wonder if on some level, I felt that that was what my mother wanted for some reason.

CBS aired a play called 6 *Rms Riv Vu*, about two married strangers who meet in an empty apartment they are both looking at. It was very poignant and starred Carol Burnett. It was so strange to see her not be Carol Burnett.

My mother was now a career counselor at Kean, a local community college. She brought home people's résumés every night and sat in the living room, rewriting them for hours.

Everything seemed to weigh on my mother. Anything at all was a burden.

WE DIDN'T have an electric lawn mower. Our lawn mower got older and older and rustier and rustier until finally you had to be a superhero to mow our lawn.

Thankfully, there was only a tiny front lawn. Nothing really grew in the backyard, so a truck came and dumped woodchips over the part that wasn't cement.

We had a clothesline in our backyard.

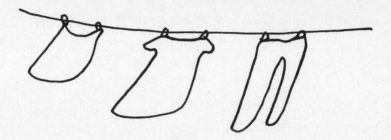

Everyone did.

WE GOT Green Stamps with our groceries at King's Market. Once or maybe twice a year, my mother sat down at the kitchen table with the stamps. I helped

her lick them and put them in square books. They tasted awful. Sometimes my mother would put out a dish of water and we would sponge the back of the stamps instead of licking them.

Then we would go to the Green Stamps store in South Orange and trade in the books for some household product, like a mixer.

All our dishes came from Green Stamps, and they were ugly.

terrible brown stripe

Come to think of it, most things from Green Stamps were ugly.

We got a digital clock from Green Stamps. It had numbers that flipped down every minute. The clock hummed at all times, then ticked as the numbers flipped. I stared at that clock as if it were a TV show. I just couldn't believe it. My mother put the clock on the dresser in my parents' bedroom, and it stayed there for more than three decades.

Every clock in my parents' house was fast. One would be eight minutes fast, another could be five minutes fast. Then we would have to spring forward or fall back and the numbers would change by a minute or two. You looked at the clocks, but you never really knew what time it was.

WE WENT to a grown-up movie every weekend or almost every weekend.

My mother always bought Jujyfruits, like a child.

Some movies had a theme song with a name, then, in parentheses, it would say it was the Love Theme from the movie. Occasionally the lead actress would sing the Love Theme, which was particularly satisfying.

The Poseidon Adventure had a great love theme called "The Morning After." Maureen McGovern sang, "There's got to be a morning after," which is true.

I loved *The Poseidon Adventure* so much that I got the book out of the library. Movies either came from books, or if they didn't, then they had novelizations that came after. I read books of many of the movies I saw and some of the television shows. *The Poseidon Adventure* was a little mature for me. There was a part in the book where the Stella Stevens character tells the Ernest Borgnine character how when she was a kid, all the neighborhood boys took her behind a fence and took turns. That was all it said. They took turns. I rolled that around and around in my head. I knew it was sexual. But what exactly did taking turns mean? It occurred to me it might mean they each had intercourse with her, but I dismissed that as it just wasn't possible. I finally decided they all took turns feeling her up. It was all very exciting in a way, but also confusing, since I lacked confidence that I really had figured it out. The one thing I knew was because it was about something sexual, I definitely couldn't ask my parents.

So first you saw the movie, then you read the book, and ideally, a little later, you read the MAD magazine version of the movie.

MAD magazine
Stella Stevens

They had a great *Poseidon Adventure*. It was called *The Poopside Down Adventure*.

We went to *The Sting*, and the movie had already started. I was beside myself. I had missed the coming attractions, plus the beginning of the movie. There was no way I was going in that theater. Somehow my parents got me to agree to go in. But when the movie ended, I refused to leave. I made everyone stay until the beginning of the next show so we could see everything we had missed.

I was a Cub Scout, then a Webelo, but never made it to a Boy Scout. Every boy I knew was a Cub Scout and every girl I knew was a Brownie. But only the weird ones became Boy Scouts or Girl Scouts. That was like going into the army.

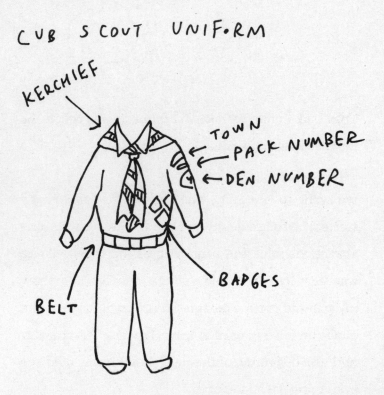

CUB SCOUT UNIFORM

KERCHIEF

TOWN
PACK NUMBER
DEN NUMBER

BADGES

BELT

MRS. BIGELOW was our Cub Scout den mother. We did little projects each week in her basement.

Once a year, there was the Pinewood Derby, where everyone took a tiny piece of wood and made it into a car, then they all raced and someone won. Fathers were supposed to help you make a Pinewood Derby racecar.

It involved sawing the block into a carlike shape, sanding it down, painting it, and adding little car decorations plus weights to make it go faster. It was totally beyond my father's capabilities. David Carcia's father had to help me make mine. I sympathize with my father. If I had to deal with making a little car for the Pinewood Derby today, I would kill myself.

MY FATHER was always worried about "the thieves" who were coming to take the things we had that had no value that were in our house.

"Did you remember to lock the door?" he would say to me or one of my brothers. "In case of the thieves."

I always had an image of a group of men that was waiting outside our house at all times, in case someone forgot to lock the door.

I GUESS he used the plural to mean one thief or another, because really our house would be a one-person job if it was any job at all. But in my mind, it was a group that all worked together in perfect unison, each assigned a complex task that only he could do, like in a heist movie.

There was not one single thing in our house worth taking. My mother had a jewelry box with a few brooches and one or two necklaces worth ten cents.

BEFORE my father went to bed every night of his life in that house, he checked the lock on the front door and then he would go down the back stairs to check the side door. The side door had a normal deadbolt lock, but also had a little latch higher up. It was just a tiny little hook on the frame, that latched into an eyehole on the door.

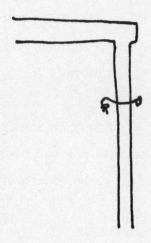

HOOK IN LATCH SO
THIEVES CAN'T GET IN

I am swearing to you that he did not spend one night in that house without also making sure that the little hook was always in the eyehole.

I wonder how that latch even got there. It was meant to be on a bathroom door (like the one that was in the tiny bathroom off our kitchen) or on a screen door (like the one on the screened front porch in the

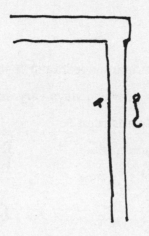

HOOK NOT IN LATCH SO
THIEVES COULD GET IN

front part of our house). There was no way this latch offered any protection from anyone. One big push and it would have come flying off the door.

Yet he had to hook the latch every night, and later, when we were teens, on the rare times that we got to use our one family car at night and were the last ones to use the side door, we had to hook the latch, too, or he would be upset.

THERE WAS an annual school fair at Tuscan. Every year, I won a goldfish. It was always very exciting to carry it home in its bag and then very sad when you flushed it down the toilet a few weeks later.

MY PARENTS would never get TV *Guide*. They acted like it was beneath them. As soon as I was old enough to get an allowance, I bought TV *Guide* every week. I went every Tuesday to the stationery store to get it the day it came out. I got it before the people who had subscriptions to it got it. I pored over it, reading every word. Once a year, there was a really special issue of

TV Guide.

It was so thick. It was like a book. Every new TV show got a page with a picture and information about it. I pored over that thing for hours.

I not only saved the Fall Preview issue of *TV Guide*. I saved every issue of *TV Guide*. I put them in boxes in the attic and would sit up there sometimes, lovingly rereading them. Sometimes instead of a photograph there would be a portrait by an artist on the cover, and that was special. I loved the portrait of Rhoda and Joe, one of television's most compelling tragic couples.

It was obvious that there was something big and exciting about each fall TV show. It wasn't like that with the midseason shows. They were more like unloved children.

Hot L Baltimore was a midseason show produced by Norman Lear, who was second only to Barbra Streisand in our house. We watched everything Norman Lear did. His shows were entertaining, but also, as my father would say, "they were about something." I loved *Maude* but never understood why she wore what she wore.

I WAS vibrating with excitement for *Hot L Baltimore*. Saul Kirschner was sleeping over at my house Friday night. *Hot L Baltimore* was premiering at nine and we were going to watch it. We talked about it all week.

Then my parents saw a commercial for it. At the end, it said that the show dealt with mature subject matter and parental discretion and judgment were advised. The male voice-over in the commercial was very serious, implying the severity of the harmfulness of not adhering to his words.

There was no way Saul and I were allowed to watch it.

"I am going to watch it," I said to my mother firmly. She explained calmly about mature subject matter and why it wouldn't be a good idea for me to see it. "I am going to watch it," I said over and over again, as she became less and less calm.

Finally, she just started crying.

In the end, I didn't watch it, and I don't think Saul even slept over.

SAUL KIRSCHNER'S mother was an artist, unlike any other parent I knew. She was a ceramicist who displayed her work on pedestals in their living room.

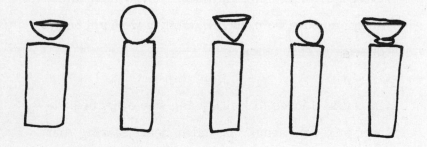

EMOTIONS were a confusing thing for me, and still are. "I'm not angry!" my father would shout, when you asked him if he was angry.

"I'm not upset!" my mother would say in an upset way, when you asked her if she was upset.

"I'm upset," I would tell my father, who would say firmly, "You're not upset."

I THINK I loved the clarity of emotions on television. Everyone was what they were. I loved how direct Ricky and Lucy were, even when they were not being direct with each other.

Of course, I loved *I Love Lucy* and saw every episode over and over again. I found it heartbreaking that Ricky got to be famous and have an exciting life at the Tropicana while Lucy was stuck in that terrible apartment with the Mertzes. Her pain was too much for me.

I guess I identified. I don't remember a time when I didn't think, *Why did I get stuck in this house?* It's not that it was such a bad house or the people were so bad. It just seemed like life was elsewhere.

I Love Lucy seemed to verify everything I could see around me and on other TV shows. New York held excitement, having glamorous places to go, like the Tropicana.

Los Angeles definitely was exciting because you could meet famous people. Those Hollywood episodes were like going to Heaven. Finally, Lucy was in a beautiful living space having fun with people like Harpo Marx, who was one of my biggest obsessions.

There was so much truth and beauty in the sequence where Lucy is dressed like Harpo—where do you begin and I end?

AND IN THE END, just like life, *I Love Lucy* got boring once Lucy and Ricky moved to the suburbs, which seemed the most accurate statement of all. They just sat in that big Connecticut farmhouse and nothing was happening, nothing at all.

It was just a lot of corny furniture.

THERE WAS a commercial on TV starring Madge the manicurist, who would be talking to her customer about how soft the dishwashing liquid Palmolive was on one's hands. In fact, she would tell the unassuming customer, "You're soaking in it right now," and the woman would pull her fingers out of the liquid with a start.

So much was happening in the Palmolive commercial. First, there was a lot of fear then about dishpan hands. You heard about it a lot, and you didn't want it. Second, the idea that something that was supposed to be harsh on your hands was instead soothing was mind-blowing. Last, there was the betrayal that Madge, someone you could trust, could have you soak your sad hands in dishwashing liquid. And she was so damn happy about the betrayal, she really was.

Maybe it had such a strong effect on me also because my mother had the saddest hands, as if she had done hard field labor her whole life.

My mother was always smiling, but her hands were the truth.

They looked like red claws. They often had white bubbles on them from where she had burned herself. "Careful! That's hot!" she constantly said to us. Yet she was the only one who ever got burned.

My mother spent so much time in the kitchen but was never at ease there. She was just getting through it.

MY MOTHER made us the thinnest sandwiches of all time—two pieces of white bread, a tiny bit of mayonnaise, and one slice of deli meat, usually bologna.

ONE OF OUR SANDWICHES

ANOTHER PERSON'S SANDWICH

IN THE BATHROOM at the Maplewood Memorial Library, there was graffiti in the stall. It said "For a Good Time call . . ." and then there was a girl's name and number. I studied that name and number every time I was in there. There was also a drawing of a penis with a mustache on it for some reason.

"For a Good Time call" this person or that was often in bathroom stalls. Once I got to high school, I occasionally knew the person the graffiti was talking about. When you saw her carrying her books down the hall, it was as if you saw someone who was famous.

No ONE I knew had a knapsack. We just carried books
in our hands.

And you covered the textbooks you got for the year
with a cut-up brown paper bag from the supermarket.
Then slowly you covered every inch of that brown
cover with doodles or words or whatever.

I WATCHED *Summer of '42* whenever it would come on.
When I was little, I saw it on the Friday Night Movie.
Then when I was older, it would be on the ABC Sunday
Late-Night Movie, which began, freakishly, at 11:45, as
if there were no rules.

Summer of '42 was about a teenager who is in love with an older married woman. They have a kind of friendship, but then she gets a telegram that her husband is killed overseas, and, grief-stricken, she sleeps with him.

Nothing seemed lighter than the clothes Jennifer O'Neill wore in that movie. It was as if they were going to fly off her at any moment.

ONCE WHEN we were on vacation, my mother was sitting on the edge of the motel swimming pool and I saw strands of hair coming out of her bathing suit.

I NEVER understood my parents' marriage. It almost seemed arranged. Marriages on TV seemed much more fun and sexy, like Bob and Emily on *The Bob Newhart Show* and Sally and Mac on *McMillan & Wife*.

THERE WAS a commercial on TV in the mornings that had pictures of extremely attractive couples doing fun things. A chorus sang, "Have a fine winter time in the Poconos, at your host with the most in the Poconos . . . Beautiful Mount Airy Lodge." There were even red bathtubs shaped like hearts for the couples.

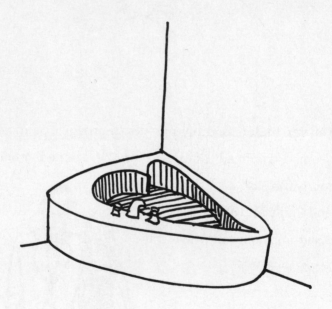

The people who got to use red heart-shaped bathtubs seemed to be leading very different lives from my parents'.

WE HAD only one working record player in the house, and that was in Michael's room. Michael got to pick his wallpaper, which had green geometric design with little mirrors in it. There were psychedelic posters on the walls. Over his bed, the members of Creedence Clearwater Revival stood in a forest, glaring at me. It smelled sort of dank in Michael's room.

I felt very adult when I sat in the big green chair that was positioned opposite the record player and listened to my music.

Once the stuffing started coming out of the chair, a big blanket was thrown over it to solve the problem.

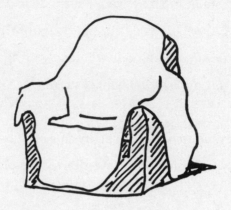

When I sat in there I felt a little nervous, as if I were assuming the role of a teenager before I was really ready, and then one day I was.

"YOU NEED something to fall back on," my mother said, when I was picking my classes freshman year of college. Both my parents insisted I take a computer class.

No one I knew at college had a personal computer. You wrote your papers on electric typewriters, or in my case, a manual typewriter.

You had to really hit those keys hard if you wanted to write anything.

It was the same typewriter both my brothers had used at college and my father had used many years before. It came in a mustard-yellow case.

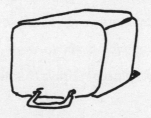

If you made a mistake on the typewriter, you used a ton of Wite-Out or used correction tape, which never really worked.

No matter how hard you tried to fix whatever you were trying to get rid of, you could always sort of see the mistake.

I LISTENED to my parents and signed up for a computer class the first week of college. Every night I went to the library that week and stared at my computer-class workbook. I am not sure what was in the workbook, because it didn't involve actually using a computer. Whatever was in there, it drove me mad. I just couldn't get my brain to understand it. Every night I left that library wanting to kill myself. Then I dropped out of computer class and felt much better. I took a course in French Surrealism instead.

NEITHER of my parents believed it was possible to get what you want. I had some painful conversation with them about doing something impractical with my life when I finally screamed, "If one person in the world is doing that job, why can't I be that person?"

Many years later, my children's preschool teacher told me the main thing you should tell your children is that you can do it.

She said, "Just keep saying those four words over and over to them. About everything. 'You can do it.' Because they can."

A FEW YEARS AGO, in a yoga class, a teacher told us all to jump up and forward from downward dog, as if we were about to take off and fly. She shrugged and said in a matter-of-fact way, "Maybe you can fly. How do we know you can't?"

And I agreed with her. We don't know we can't.

IN HIGH SCHOOL, I loved *The NBC Mystery Movie*, particularly *Columbo*. Often the villains were brilliant, creative, passionate people who were being tortured by some dullard intent on squelching their creativity or passion or essence in some way, so, like an animal, they lashed out and killed them.

I always understood and loved them.

I THINK I was petrified that I would never have a real life. Instead, I would be stuck in my parents' house forever, like they were, like everything was.

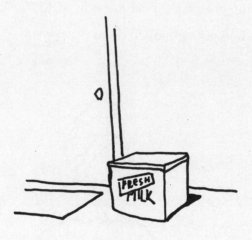

I DIDN'T FEEL confident that I would ever get out, but then when I was seventeen, the simplest thing happened and it changed everything. People started getting driver's licenses. I would be stuck in my parents' house doing whatever, and then I would hear a honk, which would mean one of my friends was outside waiting for me.

I swear that honk changed everything. You just got up and you left and you could go anywhere.

THE FIRST SUMMER after college I came home and worked in the Short Hills Mall in a children's shoe store, where I sold Strawberry Shortcake shoes.

I NEVER spent another summer at home, and even stopped coming home for school vacations during the year. I loved being on campus when everyone was gone. I love being anywhere empty. There was a commercial for Coffee-mate, a nondairy creamer, when I was a kid about a man who comes to stay in someone's apartment and discovers Coffee-mate on the shelf.

He was all alone, just him and his thoughts, and it seemed like heaven.

AFTER COLLEGE, I moved across the country to Los Angeles. The first week there, I found the palm trees unnerving, but now I think they are beautiful.

I LIVED in several apartments in Hollywood, but finally settled into one in a beautiful Spanish courtyard building, similar to where Humphrey Bogart and Gloria Grahame lived in *In a Lonely Place,* one of my favorite Channel 9 Four O'Clock Movies.

It was like I had been planning to live there my whole life.

My MOTHER retired when she was sixty-five and promptly learned she had lung cancer. She immediately got one lung removed and then started treatment.

When I was visiting her at Sloan Kettering, I took a wrong turn and I was in a hall where everyone around me had an oxygen tank.

AFTER a few months, the cancer came back and spread. It was sad that she retired then didn't get to retire.

I was visiting my parents when one night my mother had stomach pains and went to the emergency room of Saint Barnabas Medical Center. She never went home. The cancer was everywhere, and she quickly started to decline. Every day she looked worse and worse, until finally she was virtually unrecognizable from who she had been.

She brought the library book she was reading by Sue Miller to the hospital and it just sat there day after day. She never finished it.

One night I watched *Something to Talk About* with her because she wanted to. I couldn't even follow it. I still have no idea what was going on in that movie.

Whenever I think of my mother, I think first of that five-week period she was at Saint Barnabas, then I try to remember who she was before that period, for my entire thirty-four years, but it is hard.

I still wish she got to finish the Sue Miller book.

THE KITCHEN CLOCK broke sometime after my mother died. My father replaced it with a drawing of fruit. For the next decade and a half, every single time I went into the kitchen, I always looked at that drawing of fruit to see what time it was.

My FATHER was lost when my mother passed away.

About a year later, I was visiting him and opened the trunk of his car and found a pile of self-help books he had taken out of the library.

I looked at him. "Is there something you want to tell me?" I said, excited that he might want to meet a widower. He explained he was thinking about writing a book for widows from the male perspective.

Almost immediately after my mother died, my father threw himself into bereavement groups, making plans with friends, and dating. He met and fell in love with a woman named Flo. They never moved in together or married. They dated, seeing each other several times a week. My father was happy in a way I had never seen him be with my mother. Once he excitedly told me about something he and Flo had done. They went to dinner with another couple and had gotten two desserts and four forks for everyone to share them.

"Yeah," I said. "Everyone does that."

My FATHER started to find his house a burden. He spent endless hours thinking and talking about moving, but never did. The house fell into disrepair, not that it had ever really been in repair.

I visited him once and when I walked up his block, coming from the train station, I noticed the houses had fresh coats of paint, and all looked exactly as they had when I was younger. But the people who lived there were different. There was evidence of young children all around. Except at my father's house, which was originally a tan color, but that had now become gray. The gray, formerly tan, paint was peeling in places. My father was now Mrs. Soskin.

MY FATHER got prostate cancer and managed it for years. He got one protocol, then another then another.

What really seemed to bother him were his feet. He had a mysterious ailment with no treatment. Some days he would visit you with a cane, and some days he wouldn't. He could only wear enormous white sneakers.

I remember looking at him, up at the Torah at my second cousin's bar mitzvah, wearing his big white sneakers and thinking, *He looks bizarre.*

ONE DAY I called my father and found he hadn't left the house for days. In fact, he had been sleeping on the couch because he couldn't walk upstairs. I called my brother and we decided my father had to be forced to go to the emergency room.

Michael took him, and the doctor found out my father had fallen and broken his femur. When they operated they discovered he had bone cancer everywhere and had only six months to a year to live.

From the hospital, he had to go to a rehab facility in Plainfield, New Jersey. It was a bleak place and he was there for months, even though he clearly couldn't be rehabilitated in any way.

My father was depressed. Flo asked Michael to get my father's CD player clock radio and bring it to his room

so he could at least listen to the classical music CDs he loved. He did, and at the end of the evening, he went to leave and my father told him to take the CD player clock radio with him. Michael said it was for him to listen to from now on. "You can't leave it here," he snapped. "What if the thieves take it?"

I NEVER drove so much on the New Jersey Turnpike. First going to the hospital, then the rehab facility, then finally, Flo's house down by the shore, where my father lay in a hospital bed in her bedroom, tended to by a caretaker.

"Stay" by Rihanna was always on, especially if you were constantly switching between all the radio stations looking for it, as I was. I must have heard it hundreds of times on my drives down and back.

Now when I hear "Stay" it always reminds me of that time. I picture the mysterious smokestacks that line the highways of New Jersey. When I was a kid, I thought anything could be happening in those factories, and I still do.

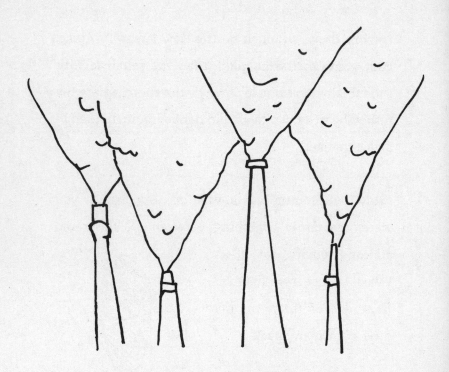

That long spring, I would sing "I want you to stay" back to Rihanna at the top of my lungs. It is only now, a year later, that I realize I was probably singing it to my father.

BOTH MY PARENTS clung to life at the end. As their bodies began to decompose, they resolutely refused to go. It was horrible to watch, yet in a way, it was amazing. I had never seen either of them fight for something before.

ONCE MY FATHER was at Flo's, he just lay in a bed.

Even though he could go outside, he had no desire
to. I would sit in Flo's bedroom, looking at the lawn
chairs in her yard, wondering why he didn't want to
feel the sun on his face.

AT FLO's, he never once mentioned the house he had
lived in for so many years, and which he knew he
would never go back to. I was stunned that he had
no interest in talking about getting rid of his things—
about who should get what, about what to throw
out.

I kept thinking, *He has this time here at the end and could
have some kind of purpose. Why doesn't he want to be in
charge of getting rid of all his things?* He could go through
everything he had accumulated over the years and let
it go. It seemed like a very profound opportunity. But
he wasn't interested.

I couldn't understand it. Ever since I was little, I have always made sure to do one thing—clean up my mess. Nothing gives me more pleasure than putting things back to how they were.

I have always wanted to get rid of all traces of my being here.

THE LAST TIME I saw my father's house, I noticed a hardened rag hanging from his bedroom window up above the front door. I wondered why he put that rag there—probably to solve some problem that putting the rag there didn't really solve.

FOR SOME REASON I didn't understand, we sold my father's house weeks before he died. I was on my way to Flo's but stopped off at my father's house because we were all supposed to take anything we wanted.

I was in a state of shock about what was happening. I remember standing in the attic, frozen, not only unable to figure out what to take but unable to have a thought. It was such a strange, unfamiliar feeling to not be able to have a thought.

I stood there forever.

Then I just grabbed my *It's a Small World* album and left the house for the last time.

ABOUT THE AUTHOR

BRUCE ERIC KAPLAN, also known as BEK, is an American artist whose single-panel cartoons frequently appear in *The New Yorker*. He also has a whole other life as a television writer and producer.